Basketball's
Half-Court Offense

BASKETBALL'S
HALF-COURT OFFENSE

JOHN CALIPARI

mp
MASTERS PRESS

NTC/Contemporary Publishing Group

Library of Congress Cataloging-in-Publication Data

Calipari, John.
    Basketball's half-court offense / John Calipari.
       p.   cm.
    ISBN 1-57028-060-6
    1. Halfcourt basketball.   I. Title. II. Series.
  GV887.C35   1996
  796.323'8—dc20   95-49685
                               CIP

Cover design by Nick Panos
Cover photograph copyright © 1997 Doug Pensinger/Allsport USA
Interior diagrams drawn by Scott Stadler
Proofread by Pat Brady

Published by Masters Press
A division of NTC/Contemporary Publishing Group, Inc.
4255 West Touhy Avenue, Lincolnwood (Chicago), Illinois 60712-1975 U.S.A.
Copyright © 1996 by John Calipari
Printed in the United States of America
International Standard Book Number: 1-57028-060-6
        03 04 05 EB 23 22 21 20 19 18 17 16 15 14 13 12 11 10 9 8

TABLE OF CONTENTS

PART 1:
MY COACHING PHILOSOPHY *1*

STYLE OF PLAY 3

EARLY OFFENSE 5

MOTION OFFENSE 7

SET PLAYS 9

ISOLATIONS 11

PRACTICE 13

DEALING WITH PLAYERS AS INDIVIDUALS 15

PART 2:
OUT-OF-BOUNDS PLAYS *21*

BEARCAT 22

BLUE 23

AWAY PLAY 24

3 PLAY 24

NEW YORK 25

LANE PLAY 25

UP PLAY 26

OVER AND UNDER PLAY 26

10 TOP 27

5 ACROSS PLAY 27

1 PLAY 28

BACK PLAY 28

2 PLAY 29

10 Play 30

Box Play 31

The Kansas 31

Double Play 32

Lob Play 33

Corner/Post Play 33

Triple Play 34

Another Possibility for the Triple Play 34

Part 3:
Half-Court Offenses 35

Wall Play 36

Post Play 37

Stack Play 38

Another Possibility for the Stack Play 38

LA 39

Hawk 40

Across Play 41

U Play 42

Zero 43

Providence 44

45 Play 45

The Regular Under 46

Regular 47

Pitt 48

UMass 49

Clear Play 50

Chicago 51

1 Out Play 52

Hand off Play 53

Away Play 54

Single Play 55

C Play 56

14 Play 57

Double Down 58

Screen/Screener Play 59

Triangle Play 60

Red Play 61

B.C. 62

Box Play 63

Triple Play 64

Zipper Play 65

Top of the Head Play 66

1 Play 67

#2 Play 68

#3 Play 69

#5 Play 70

Kansas 71

Kansas 2 71

Downscreen-Right Play 72

Downscreen-Left Play 72

Fist 73

Fist-Backdoor Play 74

Arm Out Play 75

Arm Out-Switch 75

Curl 76

X 77

1-Up Play 78

2-Up Play 79

Throwback 80

Down Play 81

Chop Play 82

Go Play 83

Baseline Play 84

Twirl Play 85

Bump Play 86

The Back 3 87

Boston 88

23 Play 89

Kentucky 90

Special 91

Jet Play 92

#4 93

Power Play 94

New York 95

Detroit 96

Motion Play 97

Quick Play 98

Acknowledgements:

Thanks to John Robic and Ed Schilling, my assistant coaches for all their help in compiling the text.

Thanks to the UMass Photographic Services for providing the photographs for the book.

Basketball's
Half-Court Offense

PART 1

MY COACHING PHILOSOPHY

STYLE OF PLAY

In my mind's eye, "UMass basketball" is five players on the floor and eight to ten others on the bench who have a burning desire to win and improve on a daily basis. They are excited about the game of basketball and see it as a part of their personal growth.

I see a selfless player who considers team success more important than individual glory. The "UMass player" understands that "as the tide rises, all the boats rise." In other words, as UMass wins, every player receives publicity and even glory. Although I have had players who could score 20 points per game, I have never had a star system. We rely on all the players to be part of our offensive and team success.

Some programs subscribe to the "buffalo mentality," meaning that there is one buffalo (a single high scorer) who leads the herd. The lead buffalo may lead the others to green pastures or off a cliff. If the lead buffalo goes to the green pasture, all the buffaloes eat well, but if the lead buffalo jumps off the cliff, well, so do the rest.

Conversely, UMass basketball has the "geese mentality," meaning we fly in formation and when the lead goose gets tired he drops back into formation and a different goose takes the lead. We do not know who is going to make the big play in a given game. The opportunity is available for any player on any night. It doesn't matter who steps up and makes the play, as long as someone does.

Although anybody can step up on a given night, we do clearly define roles that help players play to their strengths and away from their weaknesses. Every year we sit down before our first game and I tell everybody his role in front of the entire team. I specifically tell each individual what we need from him, where his shots should be taken from and where he stands at that particular point in the year.

Obviously, the roles we define can and do change as the year progresses. This past season, for example, Marcus Camby collapsed halfway through the season. When the best player goes down, everybody's role changes. Guys that were not playing many minutes had to play more, and those that were not scoring much had to shoot and score more. If players truly put out in practice on a daily basis, they are able to move from one role to a greater role with success. When we define roles, we also explain that the roles do change and may even change during the course of a game due to foul trouble or injuries. The players must therefore continue to dedicate themselves to improving. If, however, roles are not defined in a very specific manner, then teams do not reach their potential, because they do not know what is expected and the team does not play to its potential.

In addition to everybody accepting his role on our team, being the aggressor is also part of UMass basketball. I do not believe in "thuggery" basketball. Basketball that is a cross between football and mud wrestling is something that has no place in the sport that I coach. I agree with John Wooden, who sees basketball as a game of skill, finesse, speed and chemistry: five individuals working together as a cohesive unit, not five guys executing brutality. However, keeping the Wooden theory totally in place, we can still attack at both ends. I want my team to be the predator, not the prey. We want to hunt, not be hunted. We want to be on our toes and have our opponents on their heels. We don't want to be on the defensive, even when we don't have the ball.

Specifically, we implement these concepts of UMass basketball through four offensive ideas: early offense, motion offense, set plays and isolations.

EARLY OFFENSE

Early offense, or the secondary break, is one of the primary ways we become the aggressor. Our secondary break is different than most teams. I feel this if very important. By having our break different, opponents must prepare to play us. The more they have to prepare for us, the less they can prepare themselves.

Our early offense seeks to create a quick, good shot. We want to "sprint the floor to explore." Notice the word used was sprint, not run or jog. If we truly sprint we can get layups or open jump shots. If one person on the other team does not sprint back, we want them to pay. If they do get back and we don't get a good shot immediately, we swing the ball, looking for a quality shot or a post up.

We aggressively want to attack in the lane. If our secondary break is doing its job, we will win the free-throw battle. To us, winning the free-throw battle means making more free throws than our opponents shoot. Sprinting the floor in a systematic manner will make the defense react to us — hopefully, they cannot react as quickly as we can act. This reaction to us puts them a step behind and creates fouls in our favor.

MOTION OFFENSE

If we do not get a quality shot in our early offense or in swinging the ball to the other side of the court, we then go into our motion offense. The reason we run motion is to give our players the freedom to play basketball. We try to teach every player how to play, not just how to run plays. We want to make each individual better, for as each individual improves his skills our team improves. The bottom line is that the secondary break can be defended, and set plays cannot be used to score all your points. When the secondary break and set plays are cut off, that is when the players take over.

We divide our motion offense into four parts: screeners, ball handlers, post players and cutters. We break down all four components by playing two offensive players versus no defenders, then two offensive players versus two defenders, and so on until we have built up to playing four-on-four and five-on-five motion offense. It is through these breakdown drills that we do the majority of our teaching as it relates to running motion.

One element that is vital to our motion is that every player knows how to play in each part of the motion (screening, ballhandling, posting and cutting). In our motion, every player will, at some point, play every position. To take advantage of mismatches, big guys might have to be primary post passers and a guard might have to be a post-up player in a given game. We work to have all our players be competent in all four motion parts. The skills we develop in motion also prove valuable in running our set plays.

SET PLAYS

Only if our secondary break and motion offense don't get us a quality shot will we run a set play. We run early offense and motion until 20 to 25 seconds are left on the shot clock. If we don't get anything in 10 to 15 seconds, we then go to set plays. This concept is fairly unique. Most teams run a set play and if they do not get a shot from the set play, they go into motion. Again, we want to play differently than most of the other teams, making us tougher to prepare to play. Also, we believe that running motion into set plays makes the set plays a little tougher to recognize and defend. We have found that defensive players are not as eager to defend our set plays after they have been in a defensive stance for 20 or so seconds.

Additionally, our set plays are designed to get layups, not jump shots. The only time we will run a set play for a jump shot is if we need a three-pointer. Our set plays also fit our personnel. We run set plays for specific reasons. We want to take advantage of our players' strengths and talents. Running a lob play, for example, for an unathletic player is not wise. Set plays must play to your individuals' strengths and away from their weaknesses.

Further, our plays always have two or three options for different players. Our primary target might be our five man, but our two and/or four man will also have an opportunity to score. Remember our geese analogy? Our lead goose, player five, might be tired, so another goose may need to come out of formation and take the shot. Having multiple options for shots in the set play is also helpful if teams try to switch or "play the play." We have always had good success against teams that try to take away our primary target in our set plays.

Running set plays help us attack an opponent's weakness. Sometimes it is difficult for coaches to communicate the weakness we want to see exploited in our motion. However, when we signal a set play we can attack the weakness without saying a word. For example, if our opponent's five man cannot defend our five man out on the perimeter, we will simply call a set play that brings our five man outside and attack that weakness. Further, running set plays helps us keep the ball out of the hands of our players who do not have favorable matchups.

This book includes many of the set plays we have used to help us win a lot of big games. Also, it includes plays we haven't used but have picked up through scouting opponents and studying other programs. We have given you a wide sampling to get you thinking about set plays that you can adapt to fit your personnel. Don't adopt — adapt. Tailor the set plays so that they fit what you want to do, with who you have.

In a given year we run eight to 12 set plays. By the end of the year we use six to eight plays. The reason for this is that we should only run about 20 set plays in a game, the rest of the shots coming off early offense, motion and zone offenses, and pure isolations. We use the first half of the year to experiment with the plays that fit our team. As the year moves on, plays that are not producing the shots we need are weeded out. People might say that teams will scout you, so how is it possible to run only six plays? Remember, each play has two or three options and each play can only be defended a few ways and you will be able to react effectively. When we scrimmage we will have one unit do different things versus our set plays.

ISOLATIONS

Isolations are not something we use a lot; however, when the shot clock gets to five seconds you'd better have guys who can create a shot. We have a couple of things that we go to at the end of the shot clock if we didn't get anything out of our early offense, motion or set plays. We get the ball to our best creator and either clear or screen for him. We despise desperation shots and want to avoid the "hero" shot. The hero shot is the shot that is taken from about 35 feet; if it goes in, the crowd goes crazy and if it is missed, they say, "Aw! He almost made that!" Players love the hero shot because they risk nothing. They make it, they are the hero. If they miss it, well, it was an impossible shot.

As coaches we must eliminate the hero shot. A "go to" end-of-shot-clock isolation gets the ball in the right player's hands in a position where he can get off a legitimate, pretty good percentage shot. We spend time in practice working on end-of-shot-clock situations so that we have confidence in the games. Hopefully, we won't look panicked or worse, throw up the hero shot too often.

Remember, the player(s) to be isolated must work before or after practice to improve his ability to create in this one-on-one situation. Having an end-of-shot-clock play must also be in place versus a zone defense. Find a play or two that only takes seven seconds to execute for a shot and work on it in practice.

PRACTICE

In order to implement our style of play — secondary break into motion, into set plays, into an isolation — we have to give our players a crystal clear idea of how we want to play during the course of our practices. I previously touched on breaking down our motion into parts. We do our motion breakdown drills, with and without defense, every day.

Also, we run our secondary break without defense nearly every day. When we execute our secondary break without defense, we emphasize sprinting the floor and fine-tune every detail of the break, hitting a different option each time down the floor. We will go down and back two times, then the next unit does the same. We repeat this five offense versus no defense for five to 10 minutes running the secondary break into motion into our best plays. We feel this shows the players how we want to play. When we run the break into set plays we will run two or three plays for each player. I will say something like, "Run down screen for Donta with 20 seconds on the shot clock." Each player knows where he can get a shot in each set play.

Additionally, we try to go five-on-five at the end of practice for two or three segments. We break the game down into five-minute segments. Each half contains four five-minute segments. Every game we play we set the goal to win each segment. When the television time-out occurs, we immediately discuss if we won the segment. Therefore, we scrimmage in five-minute segments. After each segment we clear the score and throw the ball up again. I feel that scrimmaging this way helps us to be consistent. We don't get too high or too low in games because we don't look too far ahead — we try to look at one segment at a time.

Dealing With Players As Individuals

In working with players, I believe there are basically eight things that a coach must do on a consistent basis: be honest, be direct, define roles, show you care about your players more as people than as players, be comfortable to say "no," be fair, love them and teach them life skills.

I believe the first thing that I must do is to always be honest. For, us this honesty begins in recruiting. We never promise a player that he will start or play "x" number of minutes. Even when we recruited Marcus Camby and Lou Roe, we didn't promise that they would start. Consequently, when they did not start as freshmen they were satisfied because they were never promised a starting position. I have started six freshmen since I became the head coach at UMass, but those individuals started because they were deserving, not because I had promised them that they would. If I make promises that I do not keep, I immediately lose credibility with my players and, in turn, lose some of my effectiveness as a coach. When the coach is honest, that honesty builds trust, and trust is what keeps a team from breaking apart when adversity hits.

Being direct goes along with being honest, but it is possible to be honest and not direct. It is very easy to sugar coat things, but soft selling is dangerous. Players immediately see through the soft sell and interpret that as B.S. I feel that it is important that I be specific in what I say. Most of the time, I need to avoid general statements that, in reality, only apply to one or two guys. I need to have the guts to confront things head-on. This means being the bad guy at times. However, I believe that if I am direct and specific I will earn greater respect from my team. Ultimately, I would rather be respected than liked by my players. If I try to be liked by my team ahead of being respected, I end up with neither. But if my goal is respect, then most of the time I will get both.

The third item on my list is role definition. I spoke about this earlier. Before the first game, I call a team meeting and define each player's role as it stands at the moment. It is at that time that I boldly and directly explain specific roles. Obviously, these roles will change as the year progresses. Also, roles may change during the course of a game. Each player must, however, know exactly where he stands with the team. I have found that players would rather know where they are than to guess and be disappointed when the first game is over. When I define the roles with the team, I tell them exactly what each individual person must do for us to be successful. I also explain that if they have a problem with that role, the players need to see me immediately after the meeting.

Having each player know his role is vital in meshing the team's strengths and weaknesses. I cannot get a team to play as a unit until everybody knows what everybody is supposed to do. They may or may not like or agree with the role that I define, but they must accept it or they cannot be part of the team. If they believe they should be starting, for example, they must show me in practice and when they get into games. Even if their paying time is the last minute of the game, they have to show me they deserve more time by their performance in that one minute. How a player plays during the "mop-up" time can change his role in the next game.

Perhaps the perfect example of an individual working during practices and performing during "mop-up" time was Giddel Padilla during our 1995-1996 season. In the 1996 Final Four, we were down by 12 points against the University of Kentucky and were struggling as the game was down to the last eight minutes. I looked down the bench and caught Giddel Padilla's eyes. Giddel had only played about 40 minutes total all season, but, as we looked at each other, his eyes begged to go in the game.

Understand that one of the main reasons our guards had played so well that season was because of how hard Giddel worked all year. Giddel got the best of Edgar Padilla and Carmelo Travieso in many practices. With this in the back of my mind, and knowing how well Giddel had played in several end-of-the-game blow out situations, I sent him in the game. The lead went immediately from 12 to six due to Giddel's play. When we took Giddel out, the lead went back up for UK so we put him back in. With Giddel fighting and the others coming back to life, we cut the lead to three and had the ball and a serious chance to get to the final game. This positive situation happened because Giddel executed his role to the best of his ability all year, even when his playing time was "mop up" time and practice.

Defining roles can be a tough thing, but if the players know that you care more about them as people than you do about them as players, then they will better accept the role you define and the many other things you demand from them. It is more important to show the team that you care about them than to tell them. One of the ways I try to show them I care about each player as a person is to bring in a variety of people to talk to them about jobs after their playing career is over. I want them to feel secure that there is a job waiting for them when they are done playing ball. Also, I want to be there for my players when they need me. If they are hurt or sick, I want to be there for them. They must know that they can count on me. There are many ways to show you care, but nothing shows you care more than spending time with them. The more successful you get, the tougher finding the time becomes, but you must devote quality time to the team and its individuals. The old saying applies — "You vote with your feet."

Showing you care means sometimes saying "no." Players can ask for some wild things. Sometimes I believe that they ask to do things just to see if you care enough about them to say no. If your relationship is strong enough, then saying no isn't difficult. In fact, you need to feel comfortable in saying no. Not only must I be willing to give an unfavorable answer, but I must also be willing to follow through with my specific answers. I have to be strong enough to execute my demands and decisions.

In all situations I need to be fair. The rules for the team must be the same for everybody. However, the enforcement of the rules may be different for each individual. Running might be an effective punishment for one member of the team, but it might be painless for another. The individual who doesn't find running a punishment, might feel that getting up at 6 a.m. to study is much more severe. For some players the punishment of getting up early is tough, but for others it's no problem. As a coach, my assistants and I must have a good feel for each player on the squad. If we don't know the individuals that make up the team, then it will be difficult to assign penalties that serve the purpose we desire.

It is also important to know the most effective means for counseling each player. Some players you can scream at and it helps their play. Others, if you scream at them it tears them up and destroys their game. I get terrific results by speaking to some players in private, but no results if I say the same thing to them in front of the team. Again, we must know our team. Regardless of how we execute rule violations or how we correct the player's performance, we must always be fair. Fairness is not negotiable.

Even when I have to discipline a player, I have to love him. I am only going to be with any player on my team four years and sometimes less. I had better love him, because he will be gone quickly. Personally, I need a relationship where I can hug my players and let them know I care about them, regardless of the situation. Every player I recruit must be someone I like. I will not recruit a player that I don't enjoy being around. The reason for this is that, during the season, I am going to spend as much time with him as my own family. I want to love my players like I love my own children. Much of the joy that I have experienced as a coach is a result of my relationships and the love I have for my players, not the number of wins and championships.

The final area of managing players is teaching them life skills. I am not doing my job if I do not teach them the life skills that they need to be successful when they leave the university. I want to instill a "refuse to lose" attitude in them. What this attitude means is to play to win versus playing not to lose. Sure we may get beat on the scoreboard, but when we do, it is not because we quit trying to win. And when a team beats us, we never want to blame anybody. We never want to take a away from somebody's win. We learn from our mistakes and move on.

I explain this concept of refusing to lose often with my team. I use analogies like, "If you were selling computers and your competitor got the sale you worked hard for, would you find the guy who got the sale and punch him in the mouth? Or would you go to the person who bought the computer from your competitor and find out why you lost the sale? Was it because of your sales approach or your product? Then could you walk out, smile to your competitor and say to him that you'll see him tomorrow, knowing that you will be better?" In life, we don't win every time out, but we can learn and improve every day. We can play to win 100 percent of the time. "Refusing to lose" — teaching life skills is the lasting skill of coaching.

I hope the above seven ideas are helpful. This is not a philosophy book. It is an X's and O's book, but every coach must have a solid philosophy that he can live and coach by. A solid philosophy can cover you when the opponent's X's are bigger than your O's.

PART 2

OUT-OF-BOUNDS PLAYS

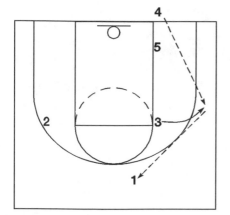

Diagram 2-1

BEARCAT

Player 3 pops to the wing and receives a pass from player 4. Player 3 hits 1 at the top. (Diagram 2-1)

Player 5 makes a circle flash through the middle of the lane. Player 4 steps in and backscreens for 3 and the lob. (Diagram 2-2).

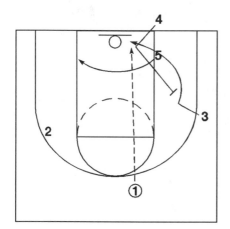

Diagram 2-2

BLUE

Player 5 pops to the corner. Player 2 hits 5.
Player 5 hits 1. Players 3 and 4 set double for
player 2 on the weakside. (Diagram 2-3)

Player 3 runs off the 4-3 double. Player 5 gets 3
in the lane. Player 1 looks for 2 or 3.
(Diagram 2-4)

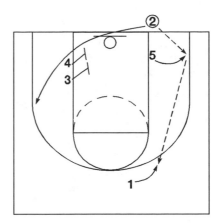

Diagram 2-3

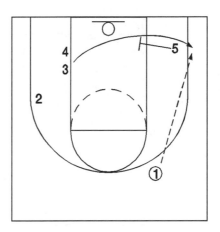

Diagram 2-4

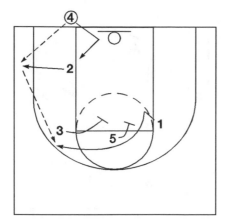

Diagram 2-5

AWAY PLAY

Player 2 pops to corner and gets the pass from 4. Player 1 runs off the staggered double by 3 and 5. Player 4 ducks in looking for the pass from 2. (Diagram 2-5)

3 PLAY

Players 1 and 2 cross off 5 at the high post. Player 4 screens up for 5 then rolls to goal. Player 5 dives to the ball. (Diagram 2-6)

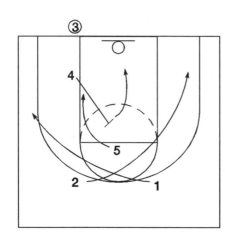

Diagram 2-6

New York

Player 5 screens for 2. Player 2 moves to the corner. Player 4 slides to the ball side wing. Player 2 hits 4. Player 1 steps in and backs-creens for 3. Player 4 looks to hit 3 for lob or hit player 1 on the pop out. (Diagram 2-7)

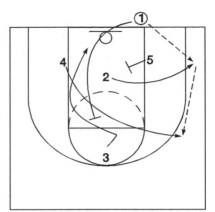

Diagram 2-7

Lane Play

Players 3 and 2 split to the blocks. Player 5 steps down and screens the middle. Player 4 slides behind 5 looking for the lob in the middle of the lane. (Diagram 2-8)

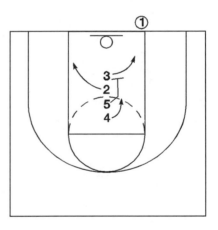

Diagram 2-8

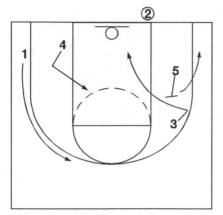

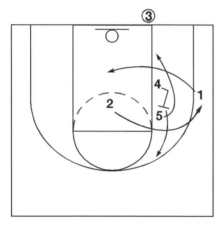

Diagram 2-9

Diagram 2-10

out-of-bounds
play **7**

UP PLAY

Spread out the set. Player 5 screens up for 3. Player 3 cuts hard either way — player 5 rolls opposite. Player 4 flashes to the lane. Player 1 outlets to the top of the key.(Diagram 2-9)

out-of-bounds
play **8**

OVER AND UNDER PLAY

Players 4 and 5 spread stack on lane. Player 1 cuts under stack. Player 2 goes over stack to wing. Player 4 steps up and screens for 5 then pops out for the outlet. Player 5 goes hard to the ball. (Diagram 2-10)

10 TOP

The players start in a box set. Player 4 pops to the corner. Player 1 hits player 4. Player 2 pops. Player 4 hits 2. Player 4 downscreens for player 1 at block then ducks in. Player 3 flashes to the lane. (Diagram 2-11)

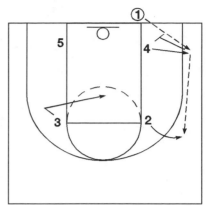

Diagram 2-11

5 ACROSS PLAY

Player 4 moves across the foul line. Player 2 curls off players 3, 4 and 5. Players 3 and 5 pinch the screen inside the foul line. Player 4 steps back for the shot. (Diagram 2-12)

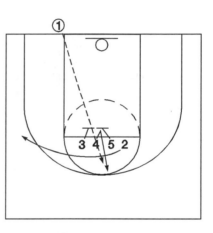

Diagram 2-12

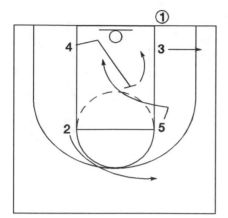

Diagram 2-13

1 Play

Players begin in a box set. Player 3 pops to the corner. Player 4 sets diagonal screen for 5 then rolls to the goal. Player 5 moves to opposite block. Player 2 moves to outlet position. (Diagram 2-13)

Back Play

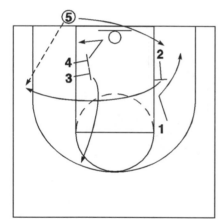

Diagram 2-14

Players 4 and 3 stack above the block. Player 2 backscreens for 1. Player 1 fades to the corner. Player 2 moves off the double. Player 3 pops back for the outlet. Player 4 ducks in. Player 5 hits 2. Player 2 looks for 4. (Diagram 2-14)

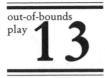

2 PLAY

The players begin in a box set. Players 3 and
5 screen across for players 4 and 2. Player 1
hits 4 in the corner. Player 4 hits 2.
(Diagram 2-15)

Player 2 takes on drag dribble to top of the
key. Players 3 and 5 set staggered double pick
or screen for player 1. (Diagram 2-16)

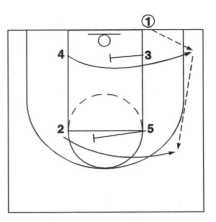

Diagram 2-15

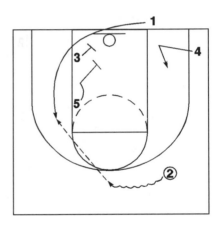

Diagram 2-16

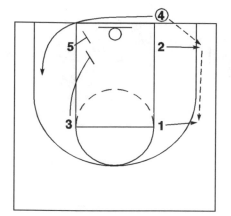

Diagram 2-17

10 PLAY

Players 1 and 2 pop out. Players 3 and 5 set a doublescreen. Player 4 hits 2. Player 2 hits 1. Player 4 goes off of doublescreen. (Diagram 2-17)

Player 1 hits 4. (Diagram 2-18)

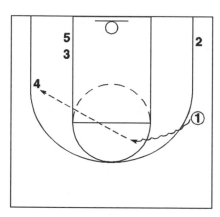

Diagram 2-18

Box Play

Players begin in a box set. Player 5 screens up for 3 at elbow. Player 3 moves to corner. Player 4 sets diagonal for 5 then rolls to goal. Player 1 moves to outlet position.
(Diagram 2-19)

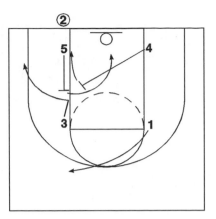

Diagram 2-19

The Kansas

Player 2 moves off 4 at elbow. Player 1 sets diagonal for 4. Player 4 goes to goal. Player 5 screens 1. Player 5 rolls to the goal.
(Diagram 2-20)

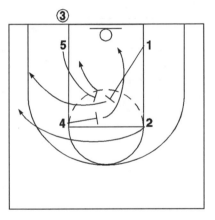

Diagram 2-20

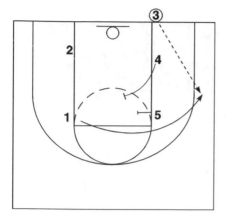

Diagram 2-21

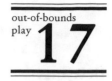

DOUBLE PLAY

Players begin in a box set. Player 1 moves off staggered double by 4 and 5. Player 3 hits 1 on the wing. (Diagram 2-21)

Player 3 ducks in on ball side. Players 4 and 5 turn and set double for 2. (Diagram 2-22)

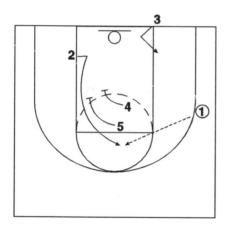

Diagram 2-22

Basketball's Half-Court Offense

LOB PLAY

Players 1 and 3 spread wide. Players 5 and 4 in lane. Player 5 drives hard to the goal. Player 4 steps anywhere to get lob. (Diagram 2-23)

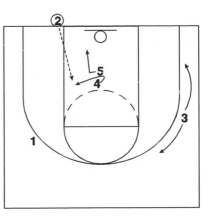

Diagram 2-23

CORNER/POST PLAY

Players 3, 4, and 5 spread across lane. Player 3 runs off 4 and 5 staggered screen. Player 1 hits 3 in the corner and goes opposite. Player 5 pops back and ducks in. Player 2 is the outlet. (Diagram 2-24)

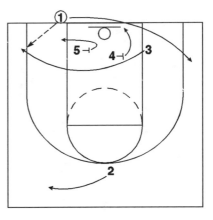

Diagram 2-24

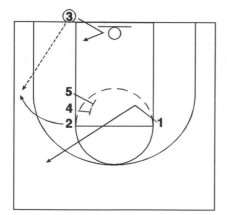

TRIPLE PLAY

Players 5, 4 and 2 stack on the lane. Players 4 and 5 set double for 1. Player 3 hits 2. Player 3 ducks in looking for pass from 2. (Diagram 2-25)

Diagram 2-25

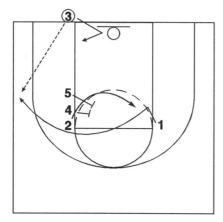

ANOTHER POSSIBILITY FOR THE TRIPLE PLAY

From the same set, player 2 can curl under the 5/4 stack to opposite block. Player 1 uses the 5/4 double . Player 3 ducks in. (Diagram 2-26)

Diagram 2-26

PART 3

HALF-COURT
OFFENSES

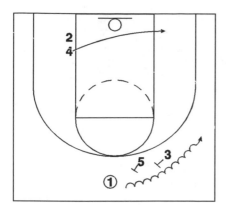

Diagram 3-1

WALL PLAY

Player 1 drives off staggered doublescreen by 5 and 3. Player 1 goes to the wing. Player 4 cuts to ballside block. (Diagram 3-1)

Player 1 looks for 4 in the post. Players 5 and 3 set a doublescreen for 2. Player 5 curls under 3 to the mid-point. Player 1 looks for 2 off the double block , 5 in the midpost or 4 on the block. (Diagram 3-2)

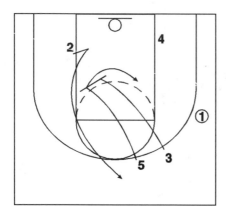

Diagram 3-2

Post Play

Players 1 and 4 are in the high set. Player 1 hits 4 in the high post. (Diagram 3-3)

Players 4 and 5 play the screen and roll at the foul line. Player 2 fades to the corner. Player 1 goes to the wing. (Diagram 3-4)

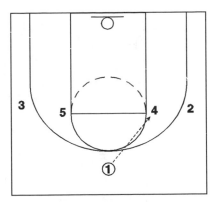

Diagram 3-3

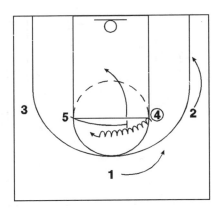

Diagram 3-4

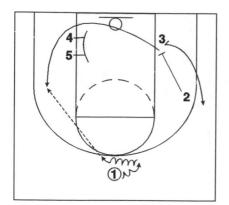

half-court
offense

3

STACK PLAY

Player 2 downscreens for 3. Player 1 drives at 3 then faces to the opposite side. Player 2 runs off the doublescreen by 4 and 5. Player 1 looks for 2. (Diagram 3-5)

Diagram 3-5

half-court
offense

4

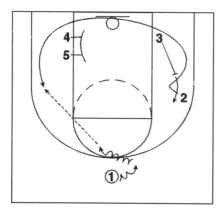

ANOTHER POSSIBILITY FOR THE STACK PLAY

From the same set, player 3 backscreens for 2. Player 3 pops to the wing for isolation. Player 2 runs off doublescreen by 4 and 5. (Diagram 3-6)

Diagram 3-6

Basketball's Half-Court Offense

LA

From a 2-3 high set, player 1 hits 4 on the
wing. Players 1 and 2 cross off 5 in the high
post. Player 3 fills in at the top. (Diagram 3-7)

Player 4 hits 3 at the top. Player 3 hits 1 on the
wing. Players 2 and 5 set double at the midpost
for 4. Player 4 makes a slice cut. Player 3
downscreens for 2. Player 2 moves to the top
of the key. (Diagram 3-8)

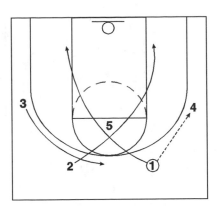

Diagram 3-7

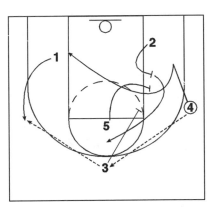

Diagram 3-8

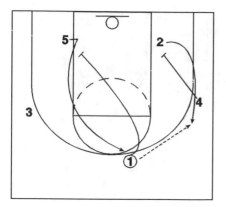

Diagram 3-9

HAWK

Player 4 downscreens for 2. Player 1 hits 2. Player 1 screens down for 5. Player 5 replaces at the top of the key. (Diagram 3-9)

Player 2 hits 5. Player 3 screens down for 1. Player 5 hits 1. Players 5 and 2 double down for 4. Player 4 curls into the lane looking for the shot. (Diagram 3-10)

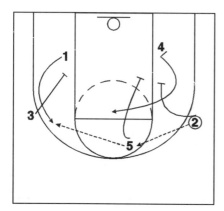

Diagram 3-10

ACROSS PLAY

From the 1-4 set, Player 1 drives at 2 on the wing. Player 2 will set diagonal up screen for 5. Player 5 dives to the ballside block. (Diagram 3-11)

After 2 screens for 5, player 4 will screen down for 2. This can be run to either side of the court. (Diagram 3-12)

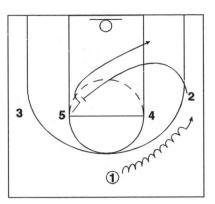

Diagram 3-11

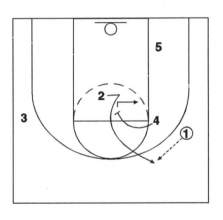

Diagram 3-12

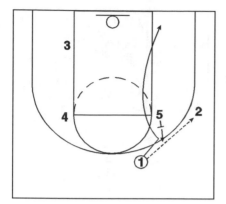

Diagram 3-13

U PLAY

Player 1 hits 2 on the wing and makes UCLA cut off 5 in the high post. Player 5 pops out. (Diagram 3-13)

Player 2 hits 5. Player 4 downscreens for 3 on the weak side. Player 1 backscreens for 2. Player 5 looks for 2 on the lob or can hit 1 on the pop out. (Diagram 3-14)

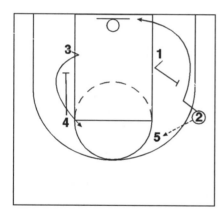

Diagram 3-14

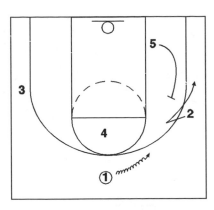

ZERO

Player 1 drives at 2 on the wing. Player 2 fades off 5. (Diagram 3-15)

Player 1 hits 2 then screens away for 3. Player 3 fills in at the top. Player 2 takes on dribble off of the staggered doublescreen by 5 and 4. Player 5 then rolls to the goal looking for post. (Diagram 3-16)

Diagram 3-15

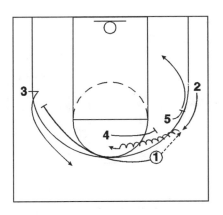

Diagram 3-16

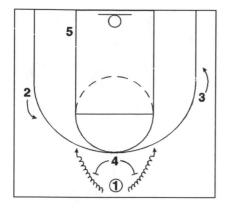

Diagram 3-17

PROVIDENCE

Player 4 sets a screen a the top of the key. Players 2 and 3 set wide, player 5 is on the block. Player 1 can go either way off the screen. (Diagram 3-17)

Player 4 can step back for spot up. Players 2 and 3 spot up on the wing. This is ideal for a last second shot at the half of a game. (Diagram 3-18)

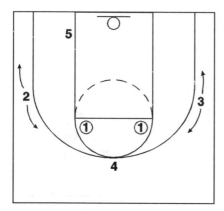

Diagram 3-18

45 PLAY

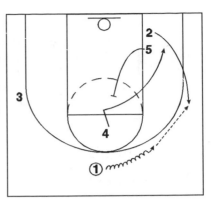

Player 1 hits 2 who pops out on the wing. Player 5 sets up the screen for 4 in the high post. Player 2 looks for 4 in the post. (Diagram 3-19)

Player 2 can hit 5 in high post and cut off 4 on the block. Player 4 will then duck in. (Diagram 3-20)

Diagram 3-19

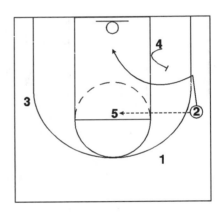

Diagram 3-20

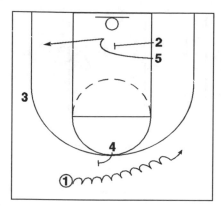

Diagram 3-21

THE REGULAR UNDER

Player 1 drives 4 at top of key. Player 5 runs off the screen by 2 to the wing. (Diagram 3-21)

Player 1 hits 3 on the wing. Player 5 steps up into the lane. Player 2 sets backscreen for 4. Player 4 will cut under on the screen to ballside dead area. (Diagram 3-22)

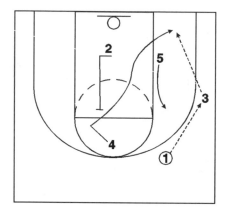

Diagram 3-22

REGULAR

Player 1 takes off the screen by 4. Player 3 runs off the screen by 2. (Diagram 3-23)

Player 5 slides up the lane. Player 2 sets a backscreen for 4 for lob or 1 hits 2 on the pop out. (Diagram 3-24)

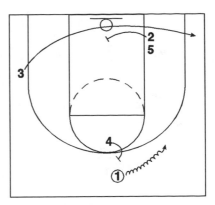

Diagram 3-23

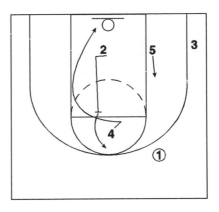

Diagram 3-24

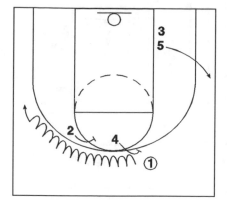

Diagram 3-25

PITT

Player 1 drives off the staggered screen by 4 and 2. Player 5 pops to the wing. (Diagram 3-25)

Players 2 and 4 double down for 3. Player 4 curls under to ballside block. (Diagram 3-26)

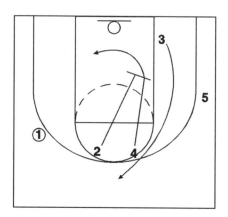

Diagram 3-26

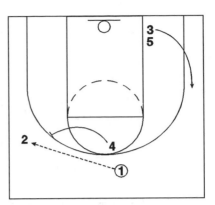

UMASS

Player 1 hits 2 on the wing. Player 3 pops to the wing. (Diagram 3-27)

Players 2 and 4 play screen and roll. Player 1 screens down for 5. Player 5 replaces at the top. Player 2 hits 5 at the top. Player 3 downscreens for 1. (Diagram 3-28)

Diagram 3-27

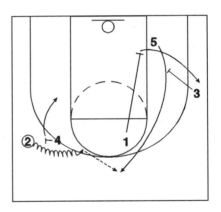

Diagram 3-28

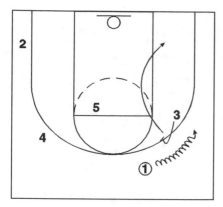

Diagram 3-29

CLEAR PLAY

Player 1 uses the screen on the ball by 3. Player 3 rolls to the goal. (Diagram 3-29)

Players 5 and 4 double away for 2. (Diagram 3-30)

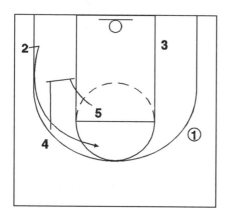

Diagram 3-30

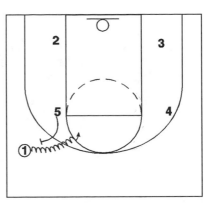

CHICAGO

Players 1 and 5 play the screen and roll on the wing. (Diagram 3-31)

Player 2 sets a backscreen for 5 on the ballside. Player 4 downscreens for 3 on the weakside. (Diagram 3-32)

Diagram 3-31

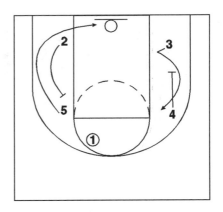

Diagram 3-32

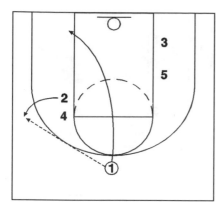

Diagram 3-33

1 Out Play

Players 2 and 4 stack at the elbow. Player 2 pops to the wing. Player 1 hits 2 and cuts to the ballside block. (Diagram 3-33)

Players 2 and 4 screen and roll on the wing. Player 2 drives off 4. Player 5 downscreens for 3 on the weakside and 4 downscreens for 1 then ducks in. (Diagram 3-34)

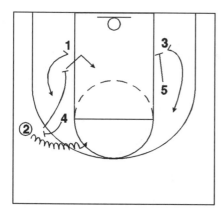

Diagram 3-34

HAND OFF PLAY

Player 1 takes on the drive and then hits 2 on the pop out. Player 5 slides to the ballside elbow. Player 3 moves to the ballside block. Player 1 gets hand off from 2. (Diagram 3-35)

Player 2 runs off the screen by 5. If the lob isn't thrown to 2, then 5 pops and gets the pass from 1. Player 1 then downscreens for 3. (Diagram 3-36)

Diagram 3-35

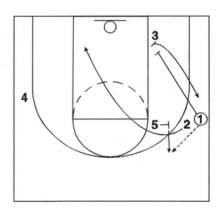

Diagram 3-36

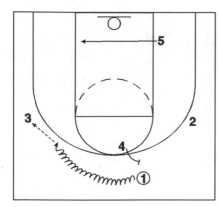

Diagram 3-37

AWAY PLAY

Player 1 uses high screen on ball by 4. Player 1 hits 3 on the wing. Player 5 chases to the ballside block. (Diagram 3-37)

Players 4 and 1 double away for 2. Player 4 then pops back to the middle of the lane. (Diagram 3-38)

Diagram 3-38

SINGLE PLAY

From the double stack low set, player 1 uses the screen on the ball by 4. Player 5 cuts to the ballside block. Player 2 curls off 3 to the weakside elbow. (Diagram 3-39)

Player 1 hits 4. Player 2 downscreens for 3 for shot. (Diagram 3-40)

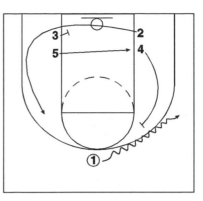

Diagram 3-39

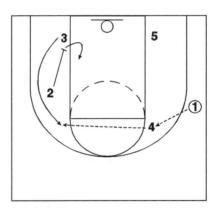

Diagram 3-40

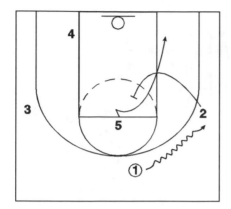

C PLAY

Player 1 takes on the drive to the right wing. Player 2 sets the zipper screen for 5. Player 5 cuts hard to the post. (Diagram 3-41)

If 5 isn't open in the post, player 1 hits 2 in the high post. Players 4 and 5 duck in. (Diagram 3-42)

Diagram 3-41

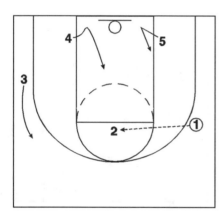

Diagram 3-42

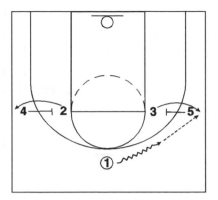

14 PLAY

Players 5 and 4 screen in for 3 and 2 at elbows. Players 3 and 2 reverse on wings, player 1 hits 3 on the wing. (Diagram 3-43)

Player 1 makes UCLA cut off 5 in the high post. Player 5 pops out. Player 3 hits 5. On the pass to 5, player 4 downscreens for 2 then ducks in. (Diagram 3-44)

Diagram 3-43

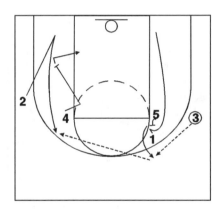

Diagram 3-44

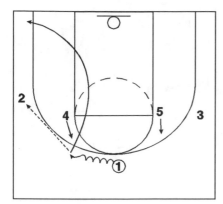

DOUBLE DOWN

Player 1 hits 2 on the wing and cuts through to ballside corner. Players 4 and 5 pop out. (Diagram 3-45)

Diagram 3-45

Player 2 reverses to 4, player 4 hits 5. Players 2 and 4 double down for 1. Player 4 slips to the post. (Diagram 3-46)

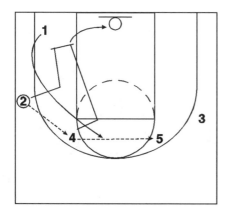

Diagram 3-46

SCREEN/SCREENER PLAY

Player 2 uses the screen on the ball by 1 and takes to the wing. Player 5 then backscreens for 1. Player 1 fades off the screen. (Diagram 3-47)

Player 3 spots up. Player 4 ducks in. Player 2 looks for 1 for shot on fade. This is a good play to use for a three-point shot for the screener. (Diagram 3-48)

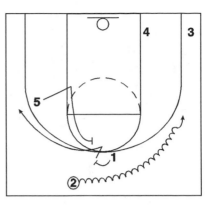

Diagram 3-47

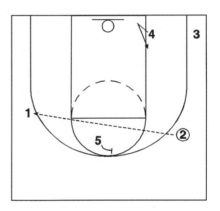

Diagram 3-48

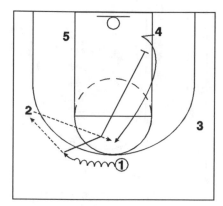

Diagram 3-49

TRIANGLE PLAY

Player 1 hits 2 on the wing then screens down for 4 on the opposite block. Player 4 replaces at the top and 2 hits 4. (Diagram 3-49)

Player 4 swings to 3. Player 1 screens away for 5. Player 4 screens down for 1. (Diagram 3-50)

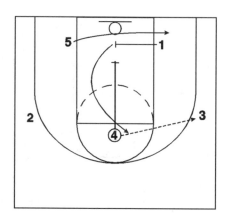

Diagram 3-50

RED PLAY

Player 1 hits 3 on the wing and uses the backscreen by 4. Player 1 goes to the ballside corner. (Diagram 3-51)

Player 4 steps out to put a screen on the ball for 3. Player 3 plays the screen and roll. Player 2 spots up the outside of three-point line. (Diagram 3-52)

Diagram 3-51

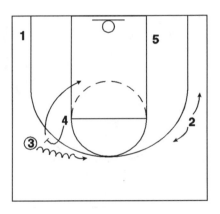

Diagram 3-52

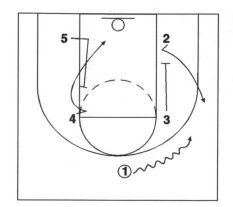

B.C.

From a box set, player 1 takes on dribble toward the wing. Player 3 screens down for player 2 on the ballside. Player 5 backscreens for 4 on the weak side. (Diagram 3-53)

Diagram 3-53

If lob to 4 isn't open, player 1 hits 5 on the pop out and 4 ducks in. (Diagram 3-54)

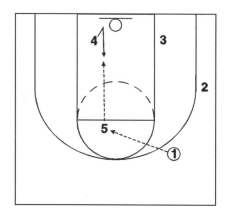

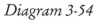

Diagram 3-54

Box Play

From a box set, players 5 and 4 downscreen for players 2 and 3. Players 2 and 3 pop to the wings. Player 1 hits 2 on the wing. (Diagram 3-55)

Player 1 screens away for 4 on the opposite block. Player 4 replaces at the foul line. Player 2 hits 4. Player 4 looks for shot or 5 on the duck-in. (Diagram 3-56)

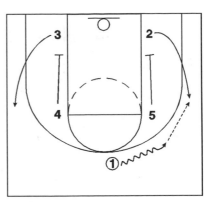

Diagram 3-55

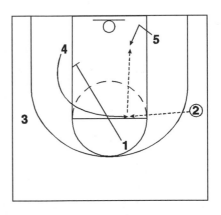

Diagram 3-56

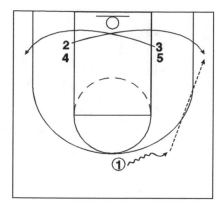

Diagram 3-57

TRIPLE PLAY

From a stack set, players 2 and 3 cross under. Player 1 drives to right and hits 2 on the wing. (Diagram 3-57)

Player 5 ducks in on the ballside. Player 1 screens down the opposite block for 4. Player 2 hits 4 in high post. (Diagram 3-58)

Player 3 screens down for 1. Player 4 hits 1 on the wing. Player 3 then screens across for 5. Player 1 looks for 5 in the post. (Diagram 3-59)

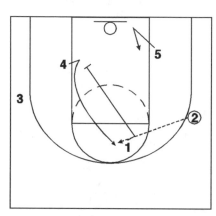

Diagram 3-58

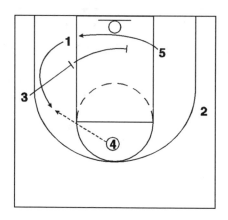

Diagram 3-59

ZIPPER PLAY

From a box set, players 4 and 5 pop out. Players 2 and 3 move to the wings. Player 1 hits 4 and cuts through middle of the lane. (Diagram 3-60)

Player 4 reverses to 2. Player 1 sets diagonal screen up for 5. Player 4 screens down for 1. (Diagram 3-61)

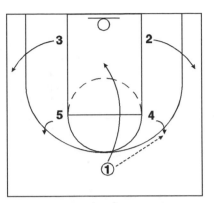

Diagram 3-60

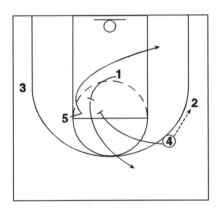

Diagram 3-61

Half-Court Offenses

65

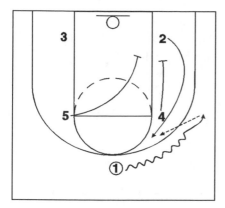

Diagram 3-62

TOP OF THE HEAD PLAY

From a box set, player 1 drives the ball to the wing. Players 5 and 4 doublescreen for 2. Player 1 hits 2. (Diagram 3-62)

Player 2 takes away on the dribble. Players 5 and 4 then set doublescreen across for 3. Player 3 curls the screen looking for pass from 2. (Diagram 3-63)

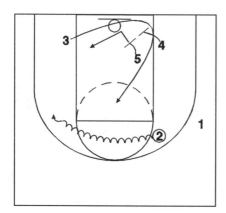

Diagram 3-63

33

1 PLAY

From a box set, player 1 takes on the dribble to the left wing. Player 5 downscreens for 3. Player 3 goes up the middle or over the top to get the pass from player 1. (Diagram 3-64)

Diagram 3-64

Player 1 hits 3. On the pass to player 3, 4 downscreens for player 2 then ducks in lane. Player 3 looks for 2 or 4 and 5 on duck-ins. (Diagram 3-65)

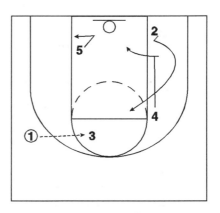

Diagram 3-65

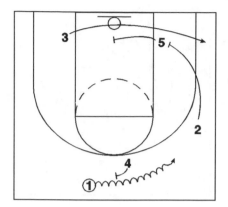

#2 PLAY

Player 1 uses high screen on ball by 4. Player 3 runs off the staggered double by 5 and 2. (Diagram 3-66)

Player 1 looks to hit 3. Player 5 turns and screens for 2. Player 4 downscreens for 2, and 1 looks for 2 at the foul line. (Diagram 3-67)

Diagram 3-66

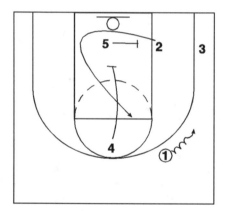

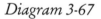

Diagram 3-67

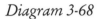

35

#3 Play

From the 2-3 high set, player 1 hits 3 on the
wing. Player 1 makes UCLA cut off 5 at the
elbow. Player 4 dives to weak side block.
(Diagram 3-68)

Player 5 pops out and gets the pass from 3.
Player 2 flares wide. Player 3 downscreens
for 1 then ducks in. Player 4 ducks in weak
side. (Diagram 3-69)

Diagram 3-68

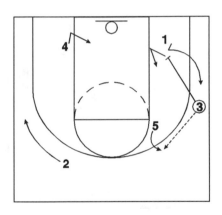

Diagram 3-69

Half-Court Offenses

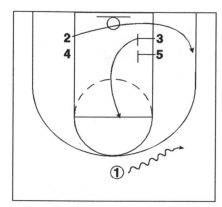

Diagram 3-70

THE #5 PLAY

From the double stack low, player 2 runs off 3 and 5's doublescreen. Player 1 takes on the dribble to the right wing. Player 3 pops to the foul line. (Diagram 3-70)

Player 1 looks to hit 3 at the foul line. Players 4 and 5 duck in the lane. Player 3 looks for a shot or 4 and 5. (Diagram 3-71)

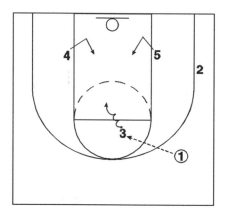

Diagram 3-71

KANSAS

Player 1 takes on the drive to the left wing.
Player 3 screens across for 5. Player 5 moves to
ballside block. Player 4 downscreens for 3.
Player 1 looks to hit 3 at the foul line.
(Diagram 3-72)

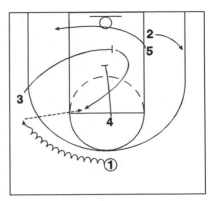

Diagram 3-72

KANSAS 2

This play uses the same basic action as the
Kansas. Player 1 takes to the left wing. Player 3
screens across for 2 instead of 5. Player 2 can
go to the corner. Player 4 downscreens for 3.
Player 1 looks to hit 3. (Diagram 3-73)

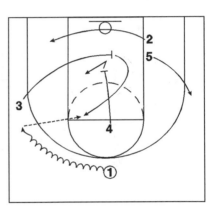

Diagram 3-73

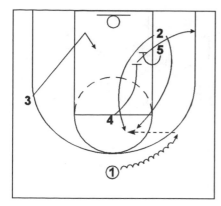

Diagram 3-74

DOWNSCREEN-RIGHT PLAY

Player 1 takes on the dribble to the right wing. Player 5 steps up and screens for 2. Player 4 screens down at the mid-post for 2. Player 2 goes either way off the staggered double. Player 4 pops to the short corner. Player 3 ducks in on the block. (Diagram 3-74)

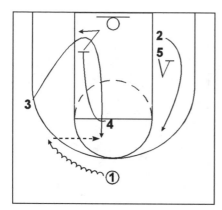

Diagram 3-75

DOWNSCREEN-LEFT PLAY

Player 1 takes on the dribble to the left wing. Player 3 takes the defender down to the block. Player 4 downscreens for 3, then ducks in. If player 1 hits 3, player 5 steps up the lane then sets downscreen for 2. (Diagram 3-75)

FIST

Player 1 hits 3 on the wing and gets in stack with player 5 at his/her elbow. Player 2 fills in for 1. (Diagram 3-76)

Player 3 hits 2 at the top. Player 3 then runs over the top of the 1-5 stack. Player 4 goes under the stack. Player 2 takes on the dribble and looks for 3 in the lane or 1 on the pop out to the top of the key. (Diagram 3-77)

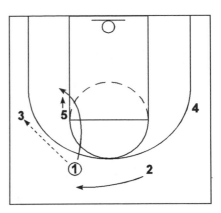

Diagram 3-76

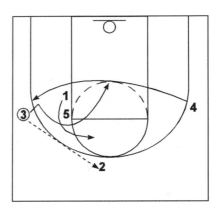

Diagram 3-77

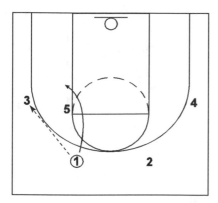

Diagram 3-78

FIST-BACKDOOR PLAY

This play uses the same basic action as the Fist. Player 1 hits 3 on the wing and stacks with 5 at his/her elbow. (Diagram 3-78)

Player 3 takes on the drag dribble. Player 4 flashes hard to the ball. Player 3 hits 4 with the pass. player 2 cuts to the backdoor looking for the pass from 4. (Diagram 3-79)

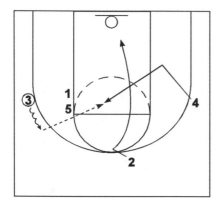

Diagram 3-79

Arm Out Play

From the box set, player 1 drives the ball to the right wing. Player 2 screens across for 3. Player 3 goes to ballside block. Players 4 and 5 set a doublescreen inside the foul line for 2. (Diagram 3-80)

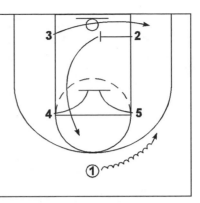

Diagram 3-80

Arm Out-Switch

From the box set, player 1 takes to the wing. Player 2 faces the screen across for 3. Players 4 and 5 set a doublescreen for 3. This option is ideal if your opponents switch to the 2-3 screen. (Diagram 3-81)

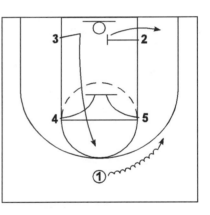

Diagram 3-81

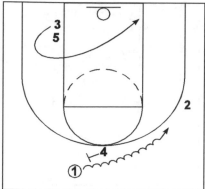

Diagram 3-82

CURL

Player 1 drives off the screen by 4 in the high post. Player 3 curls off 5 on the block. Player 3 goes to the ballside block. (Diagram 3-82)

Player 1 throws back to 4. Player 4 takes on the dribble to the wing and looks to hit 5 on the duck-in. (Diagram 3-83)

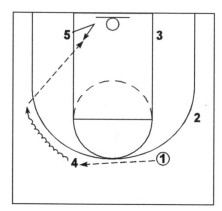

Diagram 3-83

X

From the 2-3 set, player 2 hits 3 on the wing. Players 2 and 1 cross off 4 in the high post. (Diagram 3-84)

Player 4 pops out to the top of the key. Player 3 hits 4. Player 3 downscreens for 1 then ducks in. Player 5 downscreens for 2 then ducks in. (Diagram 3-85)

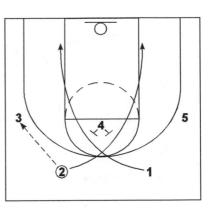

Diagram 3-84

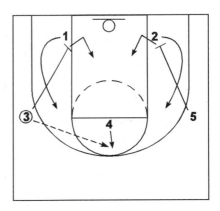

Diagram 3-85

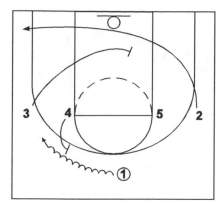

Diagram 3-86

1-UP PLAY

From the 1-4 across set, player 4 steps out and screens the ball for 1. Player 3 screens for 2 in the middle of the lane. Player 2 moves to the ballside corner. (Diagram 3-86)

Player 4 fades off 5 for a 3-point shot. Player 5 then downscreens for 3. Player 5 ducks in. This is a good play for a 3-point shot or a post up by 5. (Diagram 3-87)

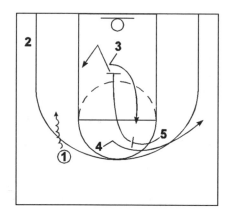

Diagram 3-87

2-UP PLAY

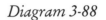

half-court offense

48

From the box set, player 2 pops out to the wing. Player 1 hits 2 then cuts to the ballside block. Player 5 pops out and gets a pass from 2. On the pass from 2 to 5, player 4 downscreens for 3. (Diagram 3-88)

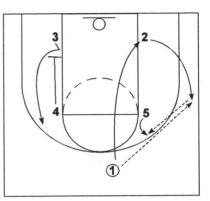

Diagram 3-88

Player 5 hits 3. Player 1 sets a backscreen for 5 for the lob. Player 4 ducks in. Player 3 looks to hit 5 on the lob, 4 on the duck-in or 1 on the pop out. (Diagram 3-89)

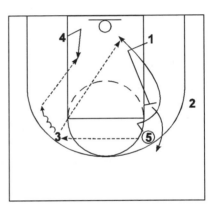

Diagram 3-89

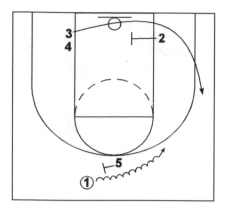

Diagram 3-90

THROWBACK

Player 1 uses a high screen on the ball by 5. Player 3 runs off the single screen by 2. (Diagram 3-90)

Player 1 looks to throw back to 5. Player 5 takes on dribble as 2 runs off the baseline screen by 4. Player 4 looks to duck in after the screen. (Diagram 3-91)

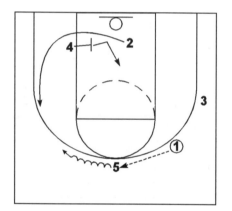

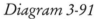

Diagram 3-91

Down Play

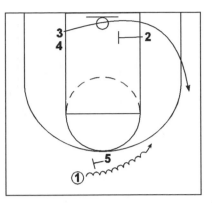

Player 1 uses a high screen on the ball by 5. Player 3 runs off the single screen by 2 to the ballside wing. (Diagram 3-92)

Player 2 then runs off the staggered screen by 4 and 5. After 4 screens for 2, player 4 ducks in. Player 1 looks for 2 off the staggered double or 4 on the duck-in. (Diagram 3-93)

Diagram 3-92

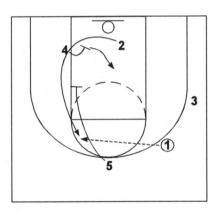

Diagram 3-93

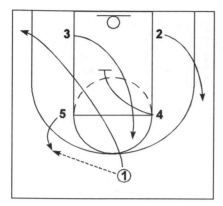

Diagram 3-94

CHOP PLAY

From the box set, player 1 hits 5 on the pop out and cuts through to ballside corner. Player 4 sets a diagonal screen down for 3. Player 2 pops wide. (Diagram 3-94)

Player 5 hits 3 then screens down for 1. Player 4 ducks in to the middle of the lane. This play is used to isolate 4 in the post. (Diagram 3-95)

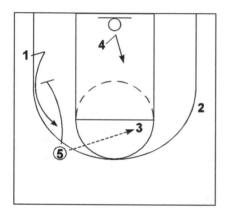

Diagram 3-95

Go Play

Player 1 uses the high screen on the ball by 5. Player 2 runs off the staggered triple screen by 4, 3 and 5. (Diagram 3-96)

Player 4 then turns and backscreens for 3. Player 3 pops to the ballside wing. Player 5 ducks into lane. Player 1 looks for 2, 3 or 5. (Diagram 3-97)

Diagram 3-96

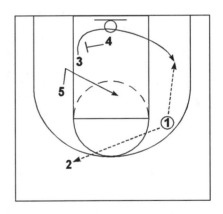

Diagram 3-97

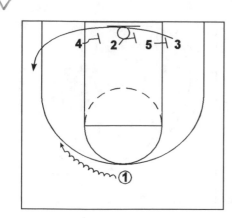

Diagram 3-98

BASELINE PLAY

From the 1-4 low set, player 1 takes the ball on a drive to the left. Player 3 runs off triple baseline screen to corner/wing. (Diagram 3-98)

If player 3 isn't open on the wing, then 1 looks for 2 off the screen by 5. Player 5 then continues across the lane and screens for 4. Player 1 hits 2, 2 looks for a shot or 4 in the post. (Diagram 3-99)

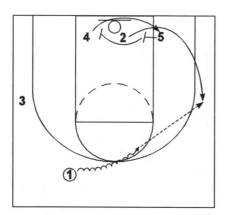

Diagram 3-99

TWIRL PLAY

Player 1 hits 2 on the wing and uses backscreen
by 5. Player 3 fills in for 1. Player 2 hits 3.
(Diagram 3-100)

Player 5 screens down for 1. Player 1 pops out
and gets a pass from 3. Players 2 and 3 interchange to take any weakside help. Player 5
steps out and screens on ball. Players 5 and 1
play the screen/roll. (Diagram 3-101)

Diagram 3-100

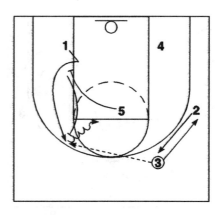

Diagram 3-101

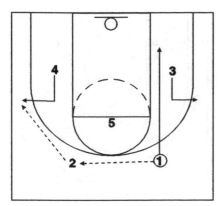

Diagram 3-102

BUMP PLAY

Players 3 and 4 walk up the lane and break out to the wing. Player 1 hits 2 and cuts to the block. Player 2 hits 4 on the wing.
(Diagram 3-102)

Player 2 runs off backscreen by 5 then off the downscreen by 5. Player 4 hits 2 at the top of the key. Player 2 takes on the dribble. Player 3 downscreens for 1 then ducks in. Player 2 looks to hit 1 or hit 3 on the duck-in.
(Diagram 3-103)

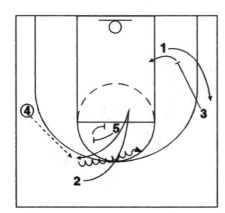

Diagram 3-103

THE BACK 3

From the box set, player 1 drives to the left wing. Player 5 sets a diagonal backscreen for 3. Player 1 looks for 3 on the lob.
(Diagram 3-104)

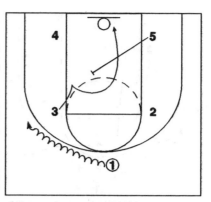

Diagram 3-104

Player 4 then backscreens for 5. Player 5 goes to a ballside block. Player 3 then backscreens for 4 on the lob. Player 2 goes to the top of the key to clear away weakside help.
(Diagram 3-105)

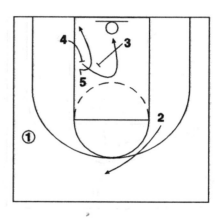

Diagram 3-105

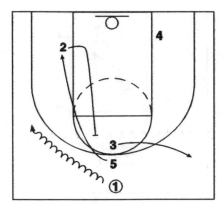

Diagram 3-106

BOSTON

Players 3 and 5 stack at the top of the key. Player 1 takes to the left wing. Player 2 backscreens for 5. Player 5 moves to ballside block. Player 3 pops out. (Diagram 3-106)

Player 1 hits 2 on the pop out. Player 4 ducks in the lane looking for a ball from 2. (Diagram 3-107)

Diagram 3-107

23 PLAY

From a wide set, player 1 takes on the dribble to the right side. Player 2 backscreens for 3. Player 3 cuts to ballside block. Players 4 and 5 set a doublescreen for 2. (Diagram 3-108)

Player 1 takes on the dribble to the right side. Player 2 fakes a backscreen then bumps back to ballside block. Player 3 runs off doublescreen by 4 and 5. (Diagram 3-109)

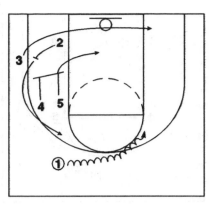

Diagram 3-108

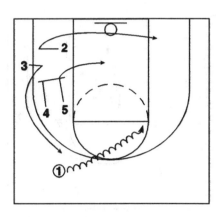

Diagram 3-109

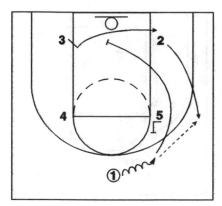

Diagram 3-110

KENTUCKY

From a box set, player 2 pops to the wing and gets a pass from 1. Player 1 makes UCLA cut off player 5 then screens across for 3. Player 3 cuts to the ballside block. (Diagram 3-110)

Player 1 then will run off doublescreen by 4 and 5. Player 2 looks for 1 off the doublescreen or 5 who slips the screen to a ballside block. (Diagram 3-111)

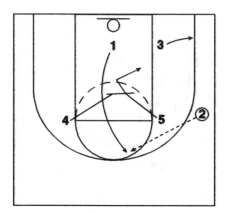

Diagram 3-111

SPECIAL

Players 2 and 3 stack at the top of the key.
Player 1 drives to the right wing. Player 4 back
screens for 3. Player 3 moves to ballside block.
Player 2 pops wide. (Diagram 3-112)

Player 3 screens across for 5. Player 4
downscreens for 3. Player 1 looks for 5 in the
post or 3 off the downscreen by 4.
(Diagram 3-113)

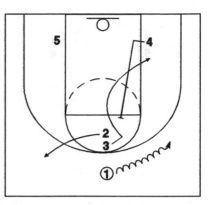

Diagram 3-112

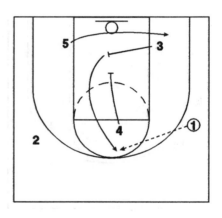

Diagram 3-113

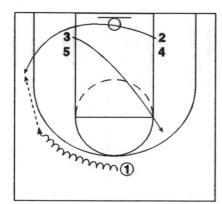

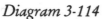

Diagram 3-114

JET PLAY

From a double stack low, player 2 runs off the double stack of 3 and 5. Player 1 takes on the dribble to the wing and hits 2. Player 3 moves to the opposite elbow. (Diagram 3-114)

Player 4 flashes from the weakside block to the ballside elbow. Player 2 hits 4. Player 4 looks to play high/low with 5. This is a good set to get into a high/low. (Diagram 3-115)

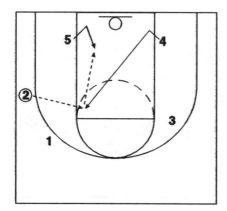

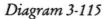

Diagram 3-115

#4

Player 1 drives to the right and hits 5 on the pop out at his elbow. Player 3 makes a slice cut off of 4 to the ballside block. Player 1 downscreens for 4. (Diagram 3-116)

Player 5 swings the ball to 4. Player 2 makes a slice cut off 3. Player 5 downscreens for 3. This is a different entry into the flex series. (Diagram 3-117)

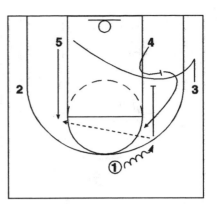

Diagram 3-116

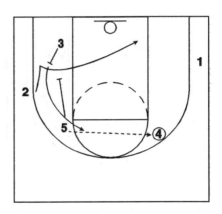

Diagram 3-117

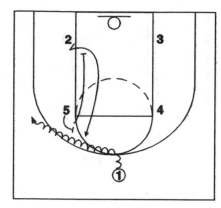

Diagram 3-118

POWER PLAY

From a box set, player 1 uses a screen on the ball at his/her elbow by 5. Player 5 then rolls and screens down for 2. (Diagram 3-118)

Player 1 looks for 5 on the duck-in or 2 for a shot. Player 4 sets downscreen for 3. Player 2 looks for 3 or 4 on the duck-in.
(Diagram 3-119)

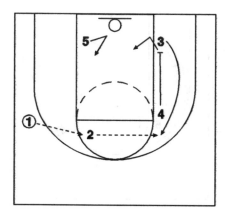

Diagram 3-119

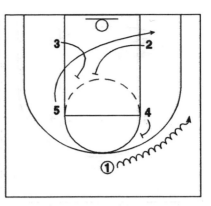

New York

From a box set, player 1 takes on the dribble off screen by 4. Players 2 and 3 set a staggered backscreen for 5. Player 5 cuts under to ballside block. (Diagram 3-120)

Player 1 looks for 5 on the block. Player 3 pops wide on weak side. Player 4 downscreens for 2 then rolls back to the ball. Player 2 pops to top of the key. Player 1 looks for 5, 4 or 2 for shot. (Diagram 3-121)

Diagram 3-120

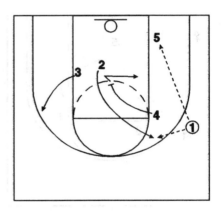

Diagram 3-121

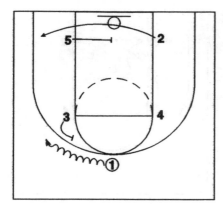

Diagram 3-122

DETROIT

From a box set, player 1 uses a screen on the ball by 3. Player 5 screens across for 2 on the baseline. (Diagram 3-122)

With player 1 on the wing, player 5 sets a backscreen for 4 looking for a lob. If 4 doesn't get the lob, he will duck in the middle of the lane. (Diagram 3-123)

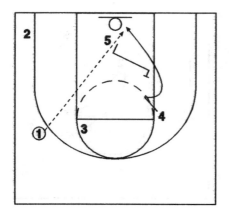

Diagram 3-123

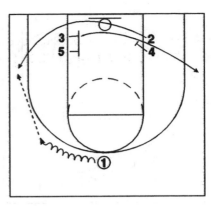

MOTION PLAY

From a double stack low, player 2 runs off the
3-5 doublescreen. Player 3 runs off the single
screen by 4. Player 1 drives the ball to the left
side and looks to hit 2 on the wing.
(Diagram 3-124)

Diagram 3-124

After 2 has the ball on the wing, player 5
screens across for 4. Player 1 and 3 interchange
on the perimeter. Run this into 3 out/ 2 in
motion game. (Diagram 3-125)

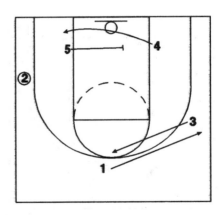

Diagram 3-125

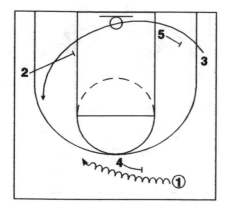

Diagram 3-126

QUICK PLAY

Player 1 uses a high screen on the ball by 4 and takes to the left side. Player 3 runs off the staggered screen by 5 and 2. (Diagram 3-126)

Player 5 then turns and screens for 2 in the middle of the lane. Player 1 throws back to 4. Player 4 looks for 2 off the screen. (Diagram 3-127)

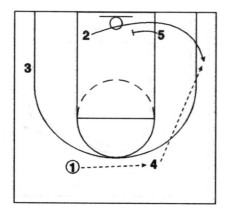

Diagram 3-127

COACHING NOTES

COACHING NOTES

COACHING NOTES

COACHING NOTES

Basketball's Half-Court Offense

COACHING NOTES

COACHING NOTES